CONTENTS

ARTICLES
1. Cantaloupe Offers More than Sweet Juicy Refreshment
2. Chard Packs a Nutritious Punch In A Colorful Package
3. Cherries Brighten the Table and Gladden the Heart
4. Coconut Cracks The Code For A Tasty Tropical Fruit
5. Collard Greens Are The Quintessential Southern Cuisine
6. Corn Offers More Than A Summer Vegetable Staple
7. Cranberries Corner the Market On Creative Nutrition
8. Cucumbers Are the Coolest In So Many Ways
9. Damson Plums Are A Delightful Discovery
10. Durian Fruit Demands Attention On Many Levels

RECIPES
1. Caribbean Chicken Cantaloupe Bowls
2. Carrot And Parsnip Whip
3. Cherries Kissed With Sabayon
4. Cherry Citrus Chicken Skillet
5. Cherry Claw-Footies
6. Cherry Hazelnut Wild Woods Rice
7. Coconut Cocoa Oatmeal Drop Cookies
8. Cool Cucumber Dressed Celery Slaw
9. Cranberry Glazed Raspberry Melon Dessert Cup
10. Cranberry Pecan Pinwheels With Orange Glaze
11. Creamy Dressed Cantaloupe Blueberry Salad
12. Crisp Coconut Shrimp with Savory Pineapple Dipping Sauce
13. Crunchy Topped Cauliflower Carrot Bake
14. Cucumber Ginger Salad
15. Curried Carrot Raisin Compote
16. Damson Plum Pudding With Butter Sauce
17. Date Walnut Sweet Bread
18. Dixie Meets Italy Collard Greens
19. Durian Fruit Puree Cheesecake
20. Garden Corn Souffle
21. Garden Cucumber Salsa
22. Kid Krazy Cabbage Casserole
23. Laotian Durian Fruit And Rice Dessert
24. Meaty Stewed Cabbage
25. Mediterranean Collards
26. Mozzarella Swiss Chard Wrap Snacks
27. Savory Sweet Cranberry Ginger Chutney
28. Sicilian Cauliflower Olio Pasta
29. Smokin Beef Celery Sticks
30. Swiss Chard Italian Lasagna

Cantaloupe Offers More than Sweet Juicy Refreshment

Some say cantaloupe and some say muskmelon. Whatever you call this pungent, juicy fruit, the fact is this is one healthy food! Cantaloupe is the perfect snack for adults and kids, and adding this fruit to your diet has definite benefits, besides just being tasty.

What is it?

Cantaloupe is part of the melon family which includes squash, cucumber, gourds, and pumpkin. In America, we know cantaloupe by its rib-textured outer skin. When you slice a cantaloupe in half, you'll find a pocket of seeds and soft threads. Scoop this out and you'll be ready to enjoy the sweet, juicy orange color flesh with its distinctive flavor and aroma.

Grown on vines, this fruit is ripe when the stem begins to separate easily from the cantaloupe itself. Because the aroma of the cantaloupe is so distinctive, many people say it is quite simple to tell if the fruit is ripe. If it smells ripe, it is ripe.

History

Christopher Columbus is credited with introducing cantaloupes to America during his second voyage to the continent in the late 15th Century. This North American cantaloupe with its familiar orange flesh is the variety we are most familiar with in America. This differs from the European cantaloupe, which has an outer rind of a gray-green color and is smooth instead of ribbed.

Long before North America was introduced to cantaloupe, Africans, Egyptians, Romans, and Greeks grew the fruit in their native lands. The varieties differed just as much as the regions, but it was all cantaloupe.

Health Benefits

Like many healthy fruits, cantaloupes are rich in vitamin C and contain antioxidants that help promote good cardiovascular health and better immunity. Cantaloupe also contains beta-carotene, a rich source of vitamin A which reduces the risk of cataracts and promotes eye health.

These vitamins also help limit the damage caused by free-radicals. We can't forget about the cantaloupe's healthy dose of B-complex vitamins which are known to help regulate blood sugar levels by processing carbs slowly, over a longer period of time.

Fun Facts

The name "cantaloupe" is derived from an Italian village called Cantalup, which was among the first places where the fruit was cultivated around the year 1700. However, this is known by a few other names in different parts of the world.

Persians and Armenians know this fruit as part of a group of muskmelons that include honeydew, casaba, and crenshaw varieties. South Africans refer to them as spanspeks. Australians call cantaloupe rockmelons.

How to Eat

Most people enjoy fresh cantaloupe raw, on its own, savoring the juicy, rich texture and flavor as a snack or dessert. However, because cantaloupe is so flavorful and appealing, many find it a fun food to experiment with in order to serve in new ways. One interesting serving suggestion is to wrap cantaloupe chunks in thinly cut prosciutto slices for a tasty and eye-pleasing appetizer.

Cantaloupe also goes well with yogurt and mixed with other fruits in sweet salads. You can even make a cold soup by blending other fruits like apples, peaches, and strawberries with cantaloupe together in a cold puree. Cantaloupe also makes a great sweet bread with just the right spices, nuts, and spices like ginger and cinnamon. Slushies and smoothies are another popular way to serve this tantalizing fruit.

Something to keep in mind is that cantaloupes have a short lifespan. Since the surface of the outer rind is so rough, it can harbor bacteria, particularly Salmonella. For this reason, it is important to wash cantaloupes well before cutting them open. Try to eat your cantaloupe within three days of purchase to reduce this bacterial risk.

The unmistakably sweet taste of ripe cantaloupe make this one fruit that is easy to enjoy. For those of us with a sense of culinary adventure, there's a world of interesting recipes waiting for you to explore with this popular seasonal fruit.

Chard Packs a Nutritious Punch In A Colorful Package

You may know chard by a number of different names, like swiss chard, spinach beet, mangold, or silverbeet. But no matter what you call it, chard is a delicious and very nutritious green. It has a wealth of nutrients and over a dozen antioxidants, making it one of the best leafy vegetables for healthy diets.

What is it?

Chard is a cousin of the beet. However, only the stalks and leaves of chard are edible, even though, like beets, they have a bulb that grows beneath the surface of the ground.

The green leaves are saturated with a deep red and white tint. The stalks of the chard plant can range in color between orange, white, red, and yellow. A variety of chard can sometimes be found packaged together as rainbow chard.

History

Ancient Greeks and Romans used chard for medicinal purposes as early as the fourth century B.C. It is native to the Mediterranean region, found mostly in Italy, France, and Spain, but is now also grown in America.

The word Swiss was added to the word chard by 19th century seed catalogs to help distinguish this vegetable from the French spinach varieties.

Health Benefits

Chard is considered one of the world's healthiest vegetables for several reasons. It has at least thirteen known antioxidants, including syringic acid, which helps regulate blood sugar levels, and kaempferol, known for its ability to benefit cardiovascular health. The stems and veins of the plant also have nutrients called betalains that help reduce inflammation and detoxify the body.

As if that's not enough, chard is an excellent source of vitamins K, A, and C, as well as a long list of nutrients that includes, calcium, iron, zinc, and phosphorus. Chard is also low in fat and cholesterol, and contains protein and dietary fiber. This very common green leafy vegetable is actually quite unique for its arsenal of healthy benefits.

Fun Facts

The word "chard" actually comes from the Latin word carduus which means thistle. As this "carduus" was being heavily cultivated in France, the word evolved into the French word "carde" which in English evolved into "chard."

Another source indicates that the word "chard" was adopted by the French in order to distinguish it from a similar celery-like vegetable called cardoon. No matter what you call it, chard certainly has developed somewhat of an identity crisis.

How to Eat

Like many other leafy greens like kale and spinach, chard can be sautéed, grilled, roasted, or steamed as a side dish of its own or as an ingredient in casseroles mixed with rice, quinoa, or pasta. You can eat the younger plants raw, but it has somewhat of a bitter taste that may be too harsh-tasting for most people.

Lots of Mediterranean dishes feature chard as part of the recipe. If stored properly in the refrigerator, chard can last up to two weeks. One of the best ways to cook chard is to boil it in a similar way you would other greens, making a traditional Southern dish that has a long history in America. Another simple recipe is to saute quickly in a skillet and toss it with some lemon juice, olive oil, and garlic.

Vegetarians frequently use chard in recipes, and one healthy idea is to create a spicy vegetable tart pie using tofu, egg whites, mushrooms, and a crust made from various seeds and walnuts.

During the peak season for chard, stock up and try adding this green to soups, pasta, quiche and other baked vegetable and cheese dishes. The nutritional benefits are incredible and you'll be enjoying a time-honored member of the family of greens!

Cherries Brighten the Table and Gladden the Heart

The song says "life is just a bowl of cherries." If that's true, you can count me in! Cherries are one of the tastiest fruits you'll ever find, and one of the prettiest when placed in a bowl on a table. So, fill a bowl and check out what cherries have in store for your life.

What is it?

Cherries are part of the agricultural family that includes plums, apricots, and peaches. Like their cousins, cherries have a stone pit in the center, but because of their smaller size, these pits cause a bit more consternation. This has inspired many inventors to design mechanical cherry pitting tools.

You'll find cherries in the stores year-round, pitted and unpitted, canned and frozen, so you can enjoy eating them just about anytime in a number of savory and sweet recipes. Not only are cherries delicious and very snack-worthy, many people enjoy them for their health benefits as well. This little dynamo contains powerful antioxidants and healthy benefits for cardiovascular wellness.

History

Cherries have been cultivated since prehistoric times, making it one of the oldest known fruits in existence. Cherry trees are native to parts of Asia and Europe. However, Greek, Roman, and Egyptian civilizations knew the fruit, as well.

At least one species of cherry trees was well established in America by the time the colonists arrived. Today, four states contribute 90% of the world's cherry crop. Of the more than 1,000 varieties of cherry trees, only 10 are commercially produced for consumers.

Health Benefits

Cherries are a great source of potassium and vitamin C, but their biggest benefit is from a specific antioxidant called anthocyanins, which also gives the fruit its rich red pigment. These anthocyanins have been shown to reduce pain and inflammation in scientific studies, which in turn reduces the risk for high cholesterol, heart disease, and excess belly fat.

Other research suggests that cherries ease painful symptoms of conditions such as gout and arthritis. One particular study by an Oregon university pointed to less muscle pain in runners who participated in a long-distance relay after consuming cherry juice for the week before the race. This is a tasty trial that I know many runners wouldn't object to participating in.

Fun Facts

One of the more expensive varieties of cherry is the Rainer cherry. The reason for this is because, in general, cherries are a favorite of birds. In the case of the Rainer cherry, the birds consume most of the season's harvest before they have a chance to be picked for commercial sale, thus creating a shortage which creates a higher price tag. Cherry trees also provide food for several species of caterpillars, so you can see that when a bowl of cherries graces our table, it's dodged a lot of obstacles to get there.

Cherry trees are classified as part of the rose family. As such, cherry leaves are poisonous, unlike the fruit itself. It takes about five years before a cherry tree matures enough for the first harvest. It's estimated that the average American household consumes about five pounds of cherries each year, and each cherry tree produces enough cherries to bake almost thirty pies.

How to Eat

Fresh cherries have a short shelf life of just four days in a refrigerator, so they must be consumed quickly or frozen as soon as possible. Freezing them quickly if not consumed fresh also retains the full benefit of the antioxidants and nutrients in the fruit. Like other highly-perishable fruit such as blueberries, cherries should not be washed until you're ready to eat them. The moisture that inevitably stays trapped in the packaging and on the fruit is bacteria's best friend.

Cherries can be snacked on as is or used in any number of recipes for a tart, fresh flavor from nature. They make great additions to breakfast foods like cereal, oatmeal, pancakes, and yogurt. You can also find dried cherries, perfect for including in meat or green salads, or with a number of pasta and rice dishes.

If you buy concentrated cherry juice, you can create some exciting smoothies and spritzers for a mid-day treat or evening cooler. Of course the dessert possibilities for cherries are well known. You'll want to give cherries a try in pies, muffins, cakes, cookies, compotes, and much more. And who hasn't indulged in a chocolate covered cherry at some point in their life?

Cherries are another of the super-foods highly recommended by nutritionists for healthy benefits. A quick search for recipes will quickly introduce you to new ways to enjoy these old time favorites which have gained in popularity again. Life is just a bowl of cherries when you include these tart morsels in your meal plan.

Coconut Cracks The Code For A Tasty Tropical Fruit

Perhaps you have enjoyed shredded coconut through the years in cookies or other desserts. But, did you know this sweet treat can be enjoyed in so many other ways? Coconut is nutritious as well as delicious. Take a look at some of the delightful surprises this fruit, or nut if you wish, has for you.

What is it?

Coconuts are a member of the palm tree family, and grow in tropical climates closer to the equator, in both hemispheres of the world. They are cultivated in over 80 countries within these regions. Coconuts have several layers, and the exterior shell is a hard, fiber-like membrane that requires a sharp knife and a little work to crack.

This fruit is officially classified as a fibrous one-seeded drupe. Now, most people (unless you're a botanist) have never heard of a "drupe." A drupe is a fruit that has what we would call a "pit" which is nothing more than a hard cover that encloses the seed, like a peach or an olive. Drupes, including coconuts, have three layers which we must navigate through to enjoy what the coconut has to offer.

History

The origin of the coconut seems to be debated a bit. One palm specialist has suggested that the coconut most likely came from the Indian Archipelago or Polynesia, using one argument that there are more varieties of coconut palms in the Eastern hemisphere than in the Americas. Other scientists argue that the coconut origins can be traced to the Americas and migrated westward across the Pacific.

Portugal and Spain are the two countries that first documented seeing coconuts during the mid 16th century, describing them as resembling the faces of monkeys. Although most often associated with the Pacific islands and southern Asia in movies, art, and historical depictions, coconuts do grow in extreme southern areas of Florida, California, Hawaii, and the Caribbean.

Health Benefits

Coconut has been credited with everything from improving hair and skin quality to easing symptoms of menopause, diarrhea, and even helping wounds heal faster. Coconut's most significant quality is to aid digestion and maintain a healthy pH balance in the intestines and lessen the amount of toxin build-up.

One of the healthiest oils you can consume is coconut oil, having much less trans fat, resulting in better benefits from the Omega-3 fatty acids the oil contains. Even though the plant is high in saturated fat, it is said to help lower cholesterol and the risk for heart disease, as well as provide a natural energy boost and help people maintain a healthy body weight.

It is also believed that coconut contains lauric acid, which helps the immune system by fighting off viral, fungal, and bacterial agents in the body. Coconut milk is another way to enjoy the health benefits of this tropical treat. Many people have found the benefits of switching from other milks to coconut milk for their own particular health needs.

Fun Facts

Some countries, Malaysia and Thailand for example, train macaque monkeys to harvest coconuts much faster than humans can. In India, this plant is sacred, and is used in ceremonies as a sign of great respect for its healing qualities and its ability to reduce stress and eliminate toxins from the body.

Coconuts are referred to as the "tree of life" because every bit of the fruit is used to produce a wealth of products such as drink, food, fiber, fuel, utensils, musical instruments, and much more. As a matter of fact, coconut water was used successfully during World War II and Vietnam as a substitute intravenous solution due to wartime shortages.

How to Eat

If you are lucky enough to get a real whole coconut, you may think it's a "touch nut to crack" but it's a lot easier than you might think once you know how. Look for the three dots resembling a face. Take a sharp object, like a meat thermometer or screwdriver, and poke the holes until you find the soft one, then push it all the way in and drain the water into a glass; taste to make sure it's sweet (not oily or sour, which then you would throw the whole thing out.) If the liquid is sweet, proceed to crack the nut by first putting in a 400 degree oven for 15 minutes. When you remove it, you'll see the hard shell has cracked. Get out a hammer and smack the coconut until it splits open. Remove the shell and peel away the brown skin attached to the white meat with a vegetable peeler. You're ready to enjoy!

The coconut meat can be shredded, shaved, or diced and is most often thought of in desserts like macaroons, cookies, pies, and cupcakes. But, don't stop there! Coconut is a wonderful addition to many main dishes and sides, as well. Add shredded coconut to breading to coat shrimp, for instance. Shred, shave, or grate fresh coconut to dress up many types of salads, including green salads, rice, and quinoa. The bulk of recipes for this tropical plant are the many delicious baked desserts and sweet breads, but use your imagination to expand your use of coconut.

The uses for coconut milk are growing in popularity every day. Combine the milk with ingredients like raisins, cranberries, brown sugar, and cinnamon to create a tasty basmati rice or brown rice pudding recipe. For meat, chicken, or other main dishes, make a spicy curry with coconut cream or milk. Turn to any Thai recipe for ways to use up your coconut milk, whether poured right from the coconut itself or purchased as processed milk.

Whether you purchase a fresh coconut or processed products made from this tropical plant, you can add a bit of healthy sweetness to your diet by exploring the many recipes for this unique fruit, nut, or whatever you call it. With a little creativity, you'll find lots of new ways to use this "tough nut" and be happy you finally cracked the coconut code!

Collard Greens Are The Quintessential Southern Cuisine

When you think Southern cooking, you can't think too long before considering collard greens. This staple of the Southern diet has a long history and many fans who have perfected cooking their "collards" for generations. Let's take a little closer look at what makes these leafy greens so special.

What is it?

Collards belong to the cabbage family of leafy vegetables which, depending on the climate, can be a perennial or biennial plant. The edible leaves have a slightly bitter taste, and are best when picked small and before they are fully mature.

Even though collard greens are available all year long, they are actually at their peak in the colder months. These greens have taken a strong hold on the Southern culture of the United States, and found their way into homes for generations, much like other greens such as mustard, chard, turnip, and kale. And, collards are actually found in many other regions around the world.

History

Ancient Romans and Greeks grew and ate collard greens as early as the 4th century B.C. The American use of collards began when African slaves brought their knowledge of creating meals from the green tops of vegetables to the colonies. Often forced to use whatever leftovers they could find after the meal was made for the "big house," these slaves learned to boil up the tossed-aside green tops of the vegetables they prepared. Slow cooking with a mixture of greens, pig's feet, or ham hocks yielded a much needed meal. The juice left from cooking greens, sometimes called pot likker, or pot liquor depending on your region, was also consumed.

As these recipes started to make their way out of the slave quarters and into the plantation kitchens, the recipes were expanded and shared in what now has become a solid Southern tradition of "soul food." But this leafy green is just as well known in Brazil, Portugal, and the Kashmir region and is so nourishing that it is considered a mainstay in these areas just as it is in America's South.

Health Benefits

Collards are known for having the best ability to bind bile acids in the digestive tract for easy consumption, thereby reducing cholesterol levels in the entire body. Cooking or steaming the greens is a much better way to produce this benefit than eating raw greens. And the taste is also improved in the cooking by most people's standards.

Whenever we talk about collard greens, we have to mention the four compounds called glucosinolates. These compounds offer protection against cancer by helping detoxify and reduce inflammation in the body. Like other cruciferous vegetables such as broccoli, cauliflower, cabbage, and bok choy, these benefits make collards a highly-recommended part of healthy diets.

Fun Facts

The state of South Carolina, the second largest producer of collards, attempted to pass a bill to make collards the official Leafy Green of the state. Many people who enjoy "soul food" along with the heritage that comes along with this African-American tradition, appreciate the idea of levitating this common green to higher status. The word "collards" is derived from the word "colewort" or "cabbage plant."

In the Southern states, when a family cooks up a big pot of greens of any variety, it is lovingly referred to as a "mess of greens." The actual distinction between a pot of greens and a mess of greens all depends on the size and tradition of the family. A New Year's tradition calls for the consumption of collards and black-eyed peas to bring good luck and a prosperous year. You might also use collard greens to do everything from curing headaches to warding off evil spirits.

How to Eat

Traditionally, collards are boiled or simmered with ham, pork, or bacon, or any salty or cured meat, and often served with cornbread to complete a true Southern-style dish. Often you'll find a jar of hot sauce or pepper sauce alongside for those who feel adventurous.

The greens make a great addition to brown rice, white rice, potatoes, pasta and quinoa. Using a flavored stock with these combinations will add a richness to the dish. Collards can also be sautéed with onions and oil or bacon grease. You may like to add a bit of brown sugar or even apple cider vinegar to kick up the flavor.

In Portugal, a popular soup called Caldo Verde (green broth) is served made with collards or kale along with potatoes and onions. This soup is often served during weddings and other celebrations.

Collards are an important part of American heritage, but also around the world, and the ancient civilizations that enjoyed them are a testament to their longevity in our culinary history. These simple greens have dressed-up tables and warmed-up bellies for generations of families who learned that cooking sometimes meant inventing delicious filling dishes from what we gathered, foraged, and cultivated.

Corn Offers More Than A Summer Vegetable Staple

No other vegetable brings up the memory of summer and warm weather fun like corn. An ear of corn buttered and seasoned to your liking is just the right thing to get you in the mood for a picnic. But, there is more to corn than that summer favorite. Let's take a closer look at some of corn's better qualities and characteristics.

What is it?

Corn is the well-recognized product of stalks growing tall in vast fields that reach the horizon. The layers of broad leaves are the germinating environment for the ears themselves, and as the corn grows inside this cocoon, male and female flowers mature and release pollen as the entire plant matures.

In the United States, corn is the leading field crop by a two-to-one margin. We know what corn on the cob looks like. But, this summer picnic staple has a bigger audience than that. Corn is used to produce everything from fuel alcohol for a cleaner burning gasoline, to butters, cereals, soft drinks, and snack foods. It is also grown as feed for livestock.

History

Corn or "maize" has been grown since prehistoric times by some of the earliest civilizations in our world's history. Mayan and Olmec cultures were among the first to cultivate corn in the southern part of Mexico, and the crop began to spread through the Americas by the year 1700 B.C.

When Europeans began to travel to and settle in the Americas, they traded corn with their mother country, and corn began to be a well-known staple of diets around the world. Today, corn is produced on every continent in the world except Antarctica.

Health Benefits

Corn's most significant contributions for our health is as a source of vitamins B1, B5, and C, as well as folate, manganese, phosphorus, and dietary fiber. Folate helps reduce the risk of birth defects, heart attack and colon cancer. The B vitamins support memory function which can reduce the onset of Alzheimer's Disease.

A diet rich in whole grains, such as the grain processed from dried corn, (cornmeal and cereals, for instance) is also generally assumed to have phytonutrients to ward off disease to our organs and vital tissues. Research has also shown that eating sweet corn can support the growth of friendly bacteria in the large intestine which can help lower the risk of colon cancer. Eating corn has been long believed to add much needed fiber to our diet. That fiber can come from eating sweet corn or cornmeal.

Fun Facts

You can get creative with corn. Of course, dried cornstalks are often bundled and used to decorate homes and businesses during the fall. Also, a corncob can be treated and hollowed out to make pipes for smoking. Some farmers plant varieties of corn that grow very tall in order to create mazes for the sake of entertainment.

Scientifically speaking, the name for corn is "zea mays" which leads us to the word "maize," the traditional name by which the Native Americans called this crop. However, many cultures throughout the world have cultivated corn and called it by a variation of the word. The colors of corn may surprise you. We normally see sweet corn on the table in shades of yellow, but corn is grown in a variety of colors which include red, purple, blue, and even pink. Some of this corn is strictly ornamental, but some is edible, too.

How to Eat

Choosing a fresh ear of corn means choosing ears that have green husks that are not dried out. You can check the freshness of individual kernels by pressing on them with a fingernail. The freshest corn will emit a milky, white fluid that indicates the corn is at its peak of sweetness and flavor. The husks protect the corn, so they should only be removed when you're ready to eat the ears you've purchased. I know many stores husk the corn, trim it, and wrap it in plastic. If that's your only option, that's fine, but look for corn that is still in the husk for optimum freshness and sweetness.

The most common variety of corn is either the yellow sweet corn or the white and yellow combination colored sweet corn. You may find a variety of colors in your region, including black, blue, and violet. These darker varieties generally contain more antioxidants and protein levels and less starch than lighter color specimens. If you can't find fresh ears of dark colored corn, check out the blue corn chips. These are increasingly popular and make a beautiful, and nutritious, snack.

Frozen whole kernel sweet corn is your next best choice after corn on the cob. The corn is picked ripe, then quickly removed from the cob, blanched and flash frozen. The quality may often surpass fresh corn toward the end of the season.

There are a number of delicious cold salads you can make with corn. You'll also find corn adds a wonderful filling taste and texture to many soups, chili, and casseroles. And don't forget the corn products, like cornmeal, cornflour, cereals, and other dried corn ingredients we can cook with.

If you are a grilling fanatic, be sure to add corn to your menu. Just remove the silk, keep the husks wrapped tightly and soak in cold water. Remove and place on low grill on indirect heat until you can smell the sweet corn aroma. Remove and baste with seasoned butter for even more savory goodness.

It's no wonder corn is such a mainstay in our diet. With so much versatility, nutrition, and deliciousness, corn is going to be around for a long time.

Cranberries Corner the Market On Creative Nutrition

Many of us recognize cranberries around Thanksgiving time as that sweet-tart relish we enjoy alongside our turkey. Or maybe we slide prepared cranberry sauce out of a can or stir them into a quick bread for a tasty treat. This versatile fruit, or berry, has many healthy advantages as well as delicious options for serving. Let's take a look at what cranberries have to offer us.

What is it?

Cranberries grow on creeping shrubs or bushes in the Northern Hemisphere, particular in cooler climates. You'll see this abundant crop often grown in bog conditions in areas of Canada and the Northern United States. The berries are most often cultivated for sauces, juice, and dried fruit for consumers, as well as fresh. Cranberries are currently enjoying super-food status due to awareness of the healthy qualities they possess.

Growing cranberries in bogs, and flooding those bogs for harvest, has several advantages. At first, it was believed only that the harvesting was easier when the cranberries floated on the water, but more research has shown that cranberries floating in bogs receive more sunlight than in other methods, and the antioxidants in the berries are boosted by the additional sunshine.

History

Early American settlers made reference to natives using the berries as food and medicine as early as the mid16th century. Settlers soon adopted a taste for cranberries and used them in recipes at the time, including the traditional Autumn harvest meal or Thanksgiving. Cool weather berries were a blessing, and a life saver, offering much needed nutrition for the early settlers, and cranberries fit the bill perfectly.

Cranberries have been so important in the development of an agricultural base in the northern states that Wisconsin, which leads the nation in the production of cranberries, has named the cranberry the official state fruit.

Health Benefits

The most widely published health benefits of cranberries is the treatment for urinary tract infections in women. Specifically, the proanthocyanidins appear to provide a barrier against bacteria that causes the infection. Other studies are applying this concept to see whether the berries can also destroy bacteria that cause stomach ulcers.

Anthocyanins are powerful antioxidants that give the berries their deep red color. These antioxidants help reduce inflammation in the body as well as preventing damage from free-radicals. Cranberries are also being studied for cancer-preventing qualities.

Additionally, cranberries supply manganese, fiber, vitamin C, as well as other essential nutrients. One cautionary note is that both cranberries and blueberries contain oxalate, which is a chemical that can add to the risk for kidney stones for those with a proclivity or history.

Fun Facts

Cranberries were named by Early American settlers who held that the blossoms appeared to resemble the sandhill crane. Hence, they initially called them "crane berries." In New England, residents sometimes referred to them a "bear berries" since they often saw bears enjoying the fruit.

Originally stored and shipped in wooden barrels weighing 100 pounds each, the "barrel" standard is still used today, although the wooden barrel has been replaced with lighter freight containers. Regarding growing them in bogs, cranberries do not grow in the water, they float on the water, making them easier to harvest as well as exposing them to more sunlight as they ripen.
Cranberries are ingredients in more than a thousand food and beverage products, with only 5% of Wisconsin's crop actually sold as fresh berries, although those bags of fresh cranberries serve as a reminder every fall to enjoy this nutritional powerhouse.

How to Eat

Fresh cranberries store well frozen whole for as long as two years. When ready to use, it works best to chop up the berries while still frozen, then added directly to recipes.

Most people get their fill of cranberries from juice or sauce, particularly during the holidays. As a healthy fruit, however, the usual line-up of cookies, bread, scones, and muffins are certainly good ways to enjoy them. Cranberry chutney and relish is also delicious, as well as jam and sweet salads with other fruits like pineapple, apples, and orange juice. Keeping a bag of frozen cranberries ready and waiting will give you all sorts of incentive to experiment.

Wine made from cranberries is a very popular treat. Cranberry juice is another beverage many people enjoy. However, it's important to look for brands that add the least amount of sugar possible when including cranberry juice in your healthy diet. 100% cranberry juice is available but can be very tart and often bitter. That's why you will normally find blends of cranberry-apple juice and similar blends. Another very popular option for enjoying cranberries in your diet is the dried cranberry snack. Add a sprinkling to salads or just grab a handful right out of the bag, much like you would raisins.

Cranberries have definitely earned the super-food label, just like other colorful berries. It's easy to find ways to enjoy the health benefits with a cool crisp glass of juice or as a sweet addition to a meal or snack. Cranberries are such a versatile fruit, you won't have any trouble finding ways to incorporate them into your diet – far beyond the Thanksgiving table.

Cucumbers Are the Coolest In So Many Ways

Often considered the "Green Goddess" of the home garden, this cooling vegetable is a long time favorite for many reasons. Not only is a cucumber a refreshing snack on a hot day, it is also very versatile. You'll find cucumbers in a soothing facial masque and a jar of pickles. You can't get much more versatile than that! Let's take a look at a few facts about this humble garden favorite.

What is it?

Cucumbers are oblong, green, vine-growing members of the gourd family, belonging to the same biological group as the cantaloupe, watermelon, pumpkin, and zucchini. There are several different varieties of cucumbers, including dwarf, standard, and pickling cucumbers that are used in different recipes and as side dishes or salad ingredients. Along with these uses, you'll find cucumber as an ingredient in an increasing number of skin care products.

History

This vegetable is said to be native to India, and has been cultivated for as much as 3,000 years in Western Asia. Cucumber cultivation later spread to Greece and Italy, and believed to be embraced especially by the Romans. Later, cucumbers were introduced to China, and spread throughout Europe most likely by the Romans. There are records of cucumbers being grown in France in the 9th century and England in the 14th century. The first recorded appearance in North America seems to be around the mid 16th century.

Cucumbers have had their ups and downs. During the 1600s, there grew a concern that eating raw fruit and vegetables caused a variety of illnesses sometimes referred to simply as the "summer diseases." Many so called experts on health claimed these uncooked garden produce unsafe, especially for children. Although a strong revolution took hold around the same time to eat simple healthy foods (credit sometimes given to the Quakers), the poor cucumber still suffered from the raw vegetable prejudice. Thus the name "cowcumber" stemming from the notion that raw cucumbers were "fit only for consumption by cows." Now, of course, the cucumber is revered in even the poshest of spas!

Health Benefits

Cucumbers contain silica, which is a vital component of our body's connective tissues (cartilage, bones, ligaments, tendons, etc). Cucumber slices and juice are also used to treat various types of swelling of the skin and eyes. They also contain potassium, magnesium, and vitamin C, which are important ingredients indicated in regulating blood pressure.

Cucumbers also contain fluid that increases the ability to absorb fiber. The high water content of the vegetable is said to benefit healthy skin and complexion overall. It is also one of the best-known diuretics, promoting the secretion of urine and helping with a number of diseases of the liver, kidney, pancreas, and bladder. Even though some say because of their high water content they don't offer much nutrition, this would definitely contradict that assumption.

Fun Facts

One of the cucumber varieties is called Burpless, a commercially-grown, seedless alternative to other varieties that are reported to cause gas in some people. Another variety is the pickling cucumber, which are also commercially grown to produce uniform-sized cucumbers used specifically for pickles.

If you think someone sitting around with cucumber slices on their eyes is a bit strange, think again. Cucumbers really do reduce swelling of eye tissue. And cucumbers are not just mentioned in fancy spas or in your favorite salad. Even the Bible has information regarding this widely available food in ancient Egypt (Numbers 11:5).

How to Eat

Cucumbers are easy to prepare and enjoy. Most of the time they are included raw in recipes, but they can be cooked as well. You can remove the seeds if you slice the cucumber lengthwise and scoop them out with a spoon. Store-bought cucumbers are often waxed, so be sure to peel them before eating them.

There are, of course, a number of cucumber salads that use vinegar, yogurt, or other creamy dressings. You can puree cucumbers and other vegetables into a hearty cold soup (gazpacho). You can also stuff them with a combination of cream cheese and horseradish for a delicious summer treat. Some people even create sandwiches using cucumbers with cream cheese, mayo, vinegar, and Worcestershire sauce.

Don't forget about the relish, salsa, and pickle recipes available as condiments or side dishes. Many people enjoy pickling their own cucumbers at home, for more organic, true flavor and less preservatives. You can even make jelly from cucumbers, bake them in the oven with herbs and butter, saute them with a light panko crust, or create a delicious, rich tapenade with anchovies, capers, olives, and snack crackers. The best way to utilize cucumbers is to experiment with recipes that call for vegetables that add crunch, but don't dominate the dish.

When they say "cool as a cucumber" they aren't kidding. This is one vegetable that refreshes in so many ways. Whether you're laying a slice on your eyelids and relaxing, or nibbling on a yummy salad, cucumbers are a very cool customer!

Damson Plums Are A Delightful Discovery

Just when you thought you knew every fruit there is, along comes a new one. Well, it's not really new, but this plum is a lesser known variety than others, so it may be new to you. Let's see if we can acquaint you with this fun fruit.

What is it?

The damson is actually one of many varieties of plum. The fruit is produced from deciduous trees that blossom with little white flowers in early spring in the northern hemisphere, then the fruit is harvested in late summer to early fall.

There are several varieties of damson, each of which has a slightly different color and taste. The Shropshire damson, for instance, has a mildly acidic taste while the Merryweather damson has a sweeter flavor, more closely resembling the plums most often found in the produce aisle. It's hard to pinpoint one particular flavor of damson because they vary so much. Damsons have a soft yellow flesh and a rich indigo blue, red, or purple skin. It can be either sweet or tart, depending on which variety of the fruit you choose. Damsons all tend to be oval shaped, slightly pointy at one end.

History

Plums generally are documented as long as 2,000 years ago. Early documentation places the damson cultivation in the region surrounding Damascus, thus the name Damson, and were most likely introduced into England by the Romans. It is not known when damson plums were introduced into North America, but some site colonists most likely brought them during the first settlements.

Evidence of damsons have been found in Roman archaeological digs across England and there is even evidence of damson skins being used to produce purple dye during those ancient times.

Health Benefits

All plums are a rich source of vitamin C, and riboflavin, as well as minerals like phosphorus, copper, manganese, magnesium and potassium, They are a good source of dietary fibers which can help lower bad cholesterol and keep the digestive tract functioning well.

It is believed that just a few plums a week can help battle fatigue. The reason appears to be because plums are loaded with essential minerals which act to calm nerves and support natural sleep patterns.

Plums also possess phytonutrients which have shown to help reduce or stop the growth of breast cancer cells. Plums also may help the body absorb iron. All this while being extremely low in calories.

Fun Facts

Damson plums can be made into gin, much like sloe gin is made from a relative of the plum, the sloe berries. Sloe gin requires more sugar because damsons are sweeter than sloe berries. Another spirit made with damson plums is Slivovitz, which is a distilled drink made in Slavic countries. Some people also make a simple damson wine. Because many varieties of damson are quite tart and acidic, people found other uses than eating them right off the tree. That's why you'll find all sorts of recipes for damson fruit liqueurs, vodka, gin, and wine.

How to Eat

As mentioned, the damson eaten right from the tree can be a bit unpalatable as the skins can be quite tart. Because of this, most damsons are grown to make into jelly or jam. There are, however, at least a few varieties of damson cultivated for eating off the tree. The Merryweather and President Plum are two such damsons. A variety called Farleigh is best known as a cooking plum.

Some damson fans have developed wonderful recipes for pickling and canning. For canning purposes, the damson fruit is boiled until tender. Then, sugar and allspice can be added when the water in the fruit has been reduced. As you continue to boil the fruit, it becomes very thick and can then be poured into jars and processed.

If you choose the sweeter variety of damson fruit, you can also make a very good pie as well as a delicious compote for tarts, or mixed with cream cheese for a delightfully sweet spread for crackers. Damsons are also used to make things like chutney, cobbler, and a variation of Eve's Pudding, which is traditionally made with apples. The intense flavor of the fruit also can be taken advantage of successfully in sauces and stuffings for roast duck and other wild game who's flavor can stand up against the damson.

If you can find damson plums in your local store, it's worth giving this fruit a try. Its acidic qualities and strong flavors may perk up your next entrée or dessert quite nicely. And when your dinner guests ask what that delightfully fresh flavor is, go ahead and throw out the name Damson and see what happens. Perhaps it will spark a lively conversation and a few puzzled, but pleased, looks!

Durian Fruit Demands Attention On Many Levels

In our quest to learn about different fruits and vegetables, we have discovered an unusual fruit from the area of Southeast Asia. The fruit, known as the "king of fruits" has some very distinct qualities. Many who have become familiar with this exotic Asian fruit admit it is definitely an acquired taste, and smell. Let's take a look and see what you think.

What is it?

The durian fruit grows on trees, which begin to bear fruit after four or five years of cultivation. These trees grow anywhere between about 85 feet to 130 feet. The fruit has a tough, thorny outer husk or shell. It is is about as large as a pineapple, sometimes growing up to a foot long, with an oblong shape consisting of several "pods." The flesh, pulp, and seeds are edible at various stages of the fruit's maturity.

The edible flesh of this fruit is a pale yellow color, and has been described as having a creamy, custard texture with a mild almond type flavor. One of its most distinctive features is the odor of the fruit itself, inside the husk. It is a strong smell that many have described as offensive or overpowering, like sulfur.

History

Durian are native to Brunei, Indonesia, the Philippines, Borneo and Sumatra and are found growing wild or semi-wild in Lower Burma (Myanmar) and the Malaysian peninsula. This fruit tree is commonly cultivated in Southeastern India, Ceylon, and New Guinea. The coastal inhabitants of Malaysia, Brunei, and neighboring countries have long considered durian a delicacy that is used in many recipes.

The Western world has known this fruit for only about the last 600 years. This fruit is either loved or loathed, there seems to no middle ground. Because of that, the importation to the United States has not been aggressively pursued. When you do find durian in the States, it is often expensive.

Health Benefits

There are some important health benefits we can enjoy by eating durian fruit. It is a good source of fiber and is actually used successfully as a colon cleanser. Durian provides a wealth of minerals and vitamins, and the simple sugars in durian produce a powerful natural energy boost. Although high in fat, durian does not contain cholesterol.

Durian is rich in vitamin C as well as the B-complex vitamins. Important minerals found in durian include copper, iron, potassium, and magnesium. The iron and copper found in durian are utilized in the body to produce red blood cells, and potassium helps regulate blood pressure and promotes heart health.

Another healthy component found in durian is tryptophan. This is used by the body to create melatonin and serotonin, which you might recognize from drug commercials as relaxing agents or as natural sleeping aids, but these are found naturally in durian.

Fun Facts

The odor of a freshly opened durian fruit has been compared to the smell of natural gas. This is probably due to the high sulfur content in the fruit. This is one of those cases where the fruit tastes nothing like it smells. Be aware that people have been known to be asked to leave areas when eating durian because of the odor. This is one fruit that's best eaten at home, and probably alone.

In Singapore, the mass transit line prohibits, by law, passengers boarding with a durian in their possession. But, Singapore has also paid homage to this "King of All Fruits" by constructing a building in its honor. Don't even attempt to eat durian on an airplane.

The older the durian tree is, the higher the quality of durian it will produce. But watch out while you stand and admire those old trees. Standing underneath a durian tree can be dangerous, as falling durian fruit have been known to be fatal upon impact with the unsuspecting gawker.

How to Eat

Cutting open a durian fruit requires considerable care and attention to avoid puncturing yourself on the pointy outer layer. Look for a line, slit, or seam running lengthwise down the fruit. This is a natural opening. Take a knife, or your hands if you dare, and gently pull the fruit open at this seam. You will be separating the durian into "pods" each of which contains little pockets of a creamy substance which you can eat (but is not very sweet) and little solid fleshy, creamy fruit pieces.

Asian cultures make good use of the durian flesh in their diets, using the natural sweetness in milkshakes, ice cream, juice, and sauces. The seeds can be boiled, fried, or roasted for a healthy snack. Even the leaves and flowers are occasionally cooked and eaten in Indonesia. Durian is also sold in neighborhood shops in the form of delicious pudding, cakes, and crepes in Singapore.

Durian should be stored well sealed and away from other foods as the odor will permeate anything in the same container, such as the refrigerator. Durian and carbonated drinks do not mix well in the stomach and has been known to cause serious complications. In the United States you are most likely to find frozen durian that has been thawed. This is fine (and cheaper than fresh) just as long as the thorny spines are not dried and brittle.

If you're looking for a truly different culinary adventure, durian would definitely be something to try. Do an online search for sources and check to see if you have an Asian marketplace in your community. Yes, the popular saying about durian is it "smells like Hell and tastes like Heaven" but that's just one more reason to be inspired to try this exotic fruit... if you dare!

Caribbean Chicken Cantaloupe Bowls

2 cups cooked chicken, cut in bite size pieces
1 can (20 oz) pineapple chunks, drained, juice reserved
1/2 cup green onions, chopped
1/3 cup diced celery
1/3 cup unsalted peanuts
1/3 cup raisins
1/4 cup shredded coconut
reserved pineapple juice
3 Tbsp mayonnaise
2 to 3 tsp curry powder
1/4 tsp powdered ginger
2 medium cantaloupes

In a large bowl, toss together the chicken, pineapple, onions, celery, peanuts, raisins and coconut and set aside.
In separate bowl, whisk together the pineapple juice, mayonnaise, curry, and ginger.
Pour this dressing over the chicken salad mixture and toss together until coated well, then cover and refrigerate for at least 1 hour before preparing finished salad.
When ready to serve, wash and cut both cantaloupes in half on the equator, then scoop out the seeds and pulp and discard, then scoop out the edible flesh with a melon baller making sure you get close to the rind, but leave enough support to form a bowl.
Put the melon balls in with the chicken salad and toss well, then spoon into the cantaloupe bowls and serve immediately.
Makes enough for 4 individual salads.

Carrot And Parsnip Whip

1 pound carrots
1 pound parsnips
1 small onion
1 cup vegetable broth
1 Tbsp margarine or butter (may substitute olive oil)
1/8 tsp ground nutmeg

Peel and cut the carrots, and parsnips into 1/2 inch pieces; peel and cut the onion into 1 inch pieces.
Put the carrots, parsnips, onion, and vegetable broth in a large saucepan; bring to a boil over medium-high heat; reduce heat immediately and cover; simmer slowly for 20 to 25 minutes or until the veggies are tender.
Drain the vegetables through a colander over a bowl, reserving broth.
Put vegetables, margarine or butter, nutmeg, and 1/4 cup of the reserved broth in your food processor and 'puree' until smooth and whipped. Add more reserved broth if you want to make the puree thinner.
Serve immediately in small bowls as a side dish loaded with nutrition. The flavors will develop more if you refrigerate overnight, then just reheat slowly in a saucepan before serving.
This also may be turned into soup by just adding more reserved broth to the food processor.
This also makes a great pasta sauce. Just adjust thickness of puree and serve over hot cooked penne or other pasta, tossing to combine.

Cherries Kissed With Sabayon

6 large egg yolks
1/3 cup sugar
1/3 cup dry white wine
1/2 pint whipping cream, whipped until stiff (or 2 cups whipped topping)
2 Tbsp Grand Marnier or Mandarin Napoleon Liqueur
2 1/2 cups tart red cherries, fresh or frozen (thawed)

Put water in the bottom of a double boiler and start heating to a simmer - do not put top of double boiler in bottom yet.
In top of double boiler (not on heat) put the egg yolks and sugar, and beat well.
Pour the white wine into the egg mixture, then (when water in bottom is simmering) place the top of the double boiler into the bottom.
With double boiler on heat, whisk the mixture constantly until it thickens and forms a custard, about 4 to 5 minutes.
Immediately remove the top of the double boiler from the heat and continue whisking the custard until the mixture has cooled.
When custard is cooled, fold the whipped cream into the custard and stir in the liqueur – don't over mix.
Put cherries in little dessert dishes and spoon the mixture over the cherries.
Serve immediately.
This will make about 8 dessert servings.

Cherry Citrus Chicken Skillet

8 pieces frying chicken (any parts you prefer)
salt and pepper to taste
1/2 cup all-purpose flour
3 to 4 Tbsp high-heat cooking oil
1 (15 oz) can pitted dark cherries packed in water, drained reserving liquid
1/2 cup white sugar
1 Tbsp cornstarch
1 orange, washed (not peeled) and cut into very thin wedges
1/2 cup slivered almonds, toasted

Season the chicken with salt and pepper, then dust with the flour to coat.
Using a large heavy skillet, pour the oil in and turn heat to medium-high.
Place chicken in pan when the oil is hot, skin side down, and fry until browned, then turn over so skin is facing up and continue frying until bottom is brown. Turn heat down to medium-low, put a cover or tin foil over the skillet and let chicken cook for 20 to 30 minutes or until no more red is visible near bone. (Cooking time and temperature will depend on whether you are cooking bone-in chicken or boneless.)
Remove the chicken from the pan and make sure you have about 1/4 cup of drippings left in the pan. (If you have more, just ladle some out. If you don't have enough, just add a little water or chicken broth to make 1/4 cup of liquid in skillet.)
With skillet on medium heat, add the cherries and sugar, stirring to combine.
Dissolve the cornstarch in the reserved liquid from the can of cherries, then add to skillet and stir, cooking until sauce thickens.
Stir in the orange slices and almonds, then arrange chicken pieces in skillet, spooning some of the sauce over the tops of the chicken; cover skillet loosely and turn heat to low and simmer just to heat everything through, about 8 to 10 minutes.
This will serve 4 people with 2 pieces of chicken each. Include hot cooked brown rice and spoon sauce over the rice if desired.

Cherry Claw-Footies

1 Tbsp unsalted butter
1 1/2 pounds cherries, pitted
3 Tbsp all-purpose flour
pinch of salt
1/4 cup granulated sugar
4 large eggs
2 large egg yolks
1 cup milk
1 cup heavy cream
1 vanilla bean, split and scraped
3 Tbsp kirsch (cherry or other fruity brandy)
confectioners sugar for dusting

Preheat oven to 375 degrees and lightly butter a 10 inch, shallow dish; fill with cherries and set aside.
In a large bowl, sift flour and salt together, then add sugar.
Start gradually adding and whisking in the whole eggs, then the egg yolks, the milk, and finally the cream.
When combined, gently stir in the vanilla bean seeds and the kirsch or other sweet brandy, then whisk again to combine.
Hold a sieve over the cherries in the dish and pour the batter into the sieve and let it drain over the cherries, making sure you let it cover the whole dish.
Bake in preheated oven for 40 to 45 minutes or until the batter puffs up and gets golden brown on top.
Remove and let cool at room temperature.
Dust with the powdered sugar lightly and serve in individual dessert bowls.
May serve with a dollop of cold whipped topping or a scoop of ice cream.

Cherry Hazelnut Wild Woods Rice

1 cup wild rice
2 1/2 cups water
1/4 tsp salt
2 Tbsp pure maple syrup
1/2 cup dried cherries
1/2 cup chopped hazelnuts, lightly toasted
1/4 cup milk or cream, warmed slightly
salt to taste

In a medium saucepan, put the wild rice, water, and salt and bring to a boil over medium heat. Immediately reduce the heat and cover the saucepan, keeping the heat on a very slow simmer for about 1 1/4 hours or until the water is absorbed. (If rice is opened and tender but there is still water in the pot, just drain it and fluff the rice.)
Remove saucepan from the heat, and immediately stir in the maple syrup, cherries, hazelnuts, and milk until blended well; add salt if desired.
Serve while still warm.
Makes about 4 servings.

Coconut Cocoa Oatmeal Drop Cookies

3/4 cup (1 1/2 sticks) butter, softened
3/4 cup granulated sugar
3/4 cup light brown sugar, packed solid
2 eggs
1 tsp vanilla extract
2 cups all-purpose flour
1/4 cup cocoa
1 tsp baking soda
1/2 tsp salt
1 1/2 cups sweetened coconut flakes
1 1/2 cups rolled oats

Heat oven to 350 degrees.
Put the butter and both sugars in a large bowl and beat with electric mixer until well blended, light and fluffy.
With beater running on slow, add in the eggs and vanilla extract and mix until incorporated.
In separate bowl, blend together the flour, cocoa, baking soda and salt, then slowly add to butter mixture with beaters running until blended.
Add the coconut and oats and stir with a large spoon until mixture is well blended.
Drop dough onto ungreased cookie sheet by tablespoons and bake 8 to 10 minutes.
Remove from oven, let cool for a minute, then slide off onto a wire rack to cool completely.
This makes about 4 dozen cookies.

Cool Cucumber Dressed Celery Slaw

3 cups thinly sliced celery
2 cups finely shredded red or green cabbage
1 medium cucumber, peeled and seeded if seeds are too big
1 cup plain nonfat yogurt
3 Tbsp sugar (more or less to taste)
1 to 2 Tbsp finely chopped fresh mint

In a large bowl, toss together the celery and cabbage; set aside.
In a separate bowl, make dressing by first grating the cleaned cucumber into a strainer placed over a bowl, then pressing grated cucumber lightly with the back of a large spoon to squeeze out excess liquid; discard liquid.
Dump cucumber out of strainer and into a clean bowl, and add the yogurt, sugar, and mint, stirring until sugar dissolves.
Pour the dressing over the celery and cabbage mixture and toss well to combine.
Serve immediately or refrigerate if necessary for up to 1 hours. The salad will tend to get watery if you keep it any longer than that.
Toss again just before serving.
Makes about 4 to 6 servings as a side salad.

Cranberry Glazed Raspberry Melon Dessert Cup

1/2 cup cranberry juice cocktail
1 Tbsp sugar
2 tsp cornstarch
1/4 tsp almond extract
3 cups cantaloupe cubes or balls
1 cup raspberries
Mint leaves, optional

In a saucepan, whisk together the juice, sugar, and cornstarch, then put over medium heat and stir until thickened.
Remove from heat and add almond extract, stirring to combine.
Allow mixture to cool in refrigerator until ready to serve.
To serve, combine cantaloupe balls and raspberries in individual dessert bowls.
Pour sauce over the top and garnish with a mint leaf.
This makes 4 to 6 dessert servings.

Cranberry Pecan Pinwheels With Orange Glaze

1 package (8 oz) refrigerated crescent rolls
1/4 cup sweetened dried cranberries
1/4 cup finely chopped pecans
1 Tbsp packed brown sugar

orange glaze:
1/2 cup powdered sugar
1 Tbsp fresh orange juice
1/2 tsp orange zest

Preheat oven to 350 degrees and cover cookie sheet with parchment paper; set aside.
On a working surface covered with a piece of parchment paper, unroll the crescent roll dough in one piece out onto the parchment paper, forming a rectangle about the size of a sheet of paper. Seal the perforations in the crescent rolls by pinching closed with your fingers.
Spread the cranberries evenly over the dough, then the pecans, and finally the brown sugar. Roll the dough into a log starting at the long edge, as tightly as you can (use the parchment paper to get you started), then pinch the seam shut the best you can.
Cut log with a sharp knife into 16 pieces; you will probably flatten them somewhat so just round them up again; then arrange each piece about 2 inches apart on the prepared cookie sheet.
Bake in the preheated oven for 12 to 15 minutes or until they get golden brown.

Prepare glaze: mix powdered sugar, juice, and zest in small bowl until well blended. This should be loose enough to drizzle, but not watery.
When you remove pinwheels from oven, drizzle glaze over while they're still warm, but not hot. Serve warm.
Makes 16 pinwheels.

Creamy Dressed Cantaloupe Blueberry Salad

1 (8 oz) container vanilla low-fat yogurt
1 Tbsp lemon juice
1 1/2 tsp poppy seeds
1 tsp orange zest
1 medium size cantaloupe, cleaned and sliced into crescent shapes
24 Boston lettuce leaves
2 cups fresh blueberries

Combine the yogurt, lemon juice, poppy seeds, and orange zest in a bowl and whisk until smooth and creamy; cover and put in refrigerator to chill.
Divide the lettuce leaves between 8 chilled salad plates, then top with the sliced cantaloupe, arranging evenly between plates.
Spoon 1/4 cup of the blueberries over each salad, then drizzle the yogurt dressing over each salad and serve immediately.
Makes 8 salads.

Crisp Coconut Shrimp with Savory Pineapple Dipping Sauce

1/2 cup flour
1/2 tsp baking powder
1/2 tsp paprika
1/2 tsp garlic salt
2/3 cup water
1/2 cup bread crumbs
2 cups shredded coconut (use sweetened or unsweetened)
1 lb shrimp, peeled and cleaned

Sauce:
1 can (20 oz) pineapple chunks in juice
3 cloves garlic, peeled
2 Tbsp soy sauce
2 Tbsp cornstarch
1 red bell pepper, cleaned and chopped
2 Tbsp apple cider vinegar (may substitute lemon juice)

Start by preparing the sauce. Put pineapple chunks, including the juice, in food processor and add the garlic, soy sauce, and cornstarch and process until smooth, then add chopped red bell peppers and pulse until peppers are chopped small and blended in (you want to see the peppers but the pieces should be tiny.)
Pour this mixture into a saucepan over low heat and simmer for 10 to 15 minutes or until the sauce has thickened, then add the vinegar and stir; set aside.
(You can make this sauce ahead of time and refrigerate. It can then be served either hot or cold with your shrimp.).
To prepare batter for shrimp: Put the flour, salt, baking powder, and paprika in a bowl and mix together until blended, then pour in the water and whisk until batter is smooth; set aside.
In a separate bowl, put the bread crumbs and coconut and mix together.
To coat shrimp: Take each shrimp and first dip in batter, then roll in the coconut mixture, making sure the shrimp is well coated. Set each shrimp on a large sheet while you prepare the oil for frying.
Using a large heavy cast iron skillet, pour about 1 inch of high-heat oil (I prefer peanut oil) in the skillet and put over medium-high heat until oil sputters when a drop of water is added. If you have a candy thermometer heat to 360 to 365 degrees.
Gently place a few shrimp in the oil and cook until golden brown, flipping the shrimp once during the cooking time. Remove cooked shrimp as they brown and put on paper towel covered cooling rack to drain.

Crunchy Topped Cauliflower Carrot Bake

1 head cauliflower, broken into small florets
4 medium carrots, peeled, sliced in bite size pieces diagonally
3 egg yolks
1/4 tsp salt
2 Tbsp lemon juice
1 dash hot pepper sauce
1/2 cup butter, melted
3/4 cup coarsely crushed crackers (like Ritz)
1 Tbsp butter, melted

Preheat the oven to 350 degrees.
In a large saucepan, put the cauliflower and carrots, add water about half way up, and put over high heat and bring to a boil, turn heat down to a slow boil and cook for about 6 to 7 minutes or until vegetables are just barely fork tender. Drain well and dump into a large shallow casserole dish.
In a food processor, add the egg yolks, salt, lemon juice, and hot pepper sauce and start blending just to mix, then, with motor running, slowly drizzle in the melted butter and continue blending until sauce thickens.
Pour sauce over the cauliflower-carrot casserole.
In separate bowl, stir together the cracker crumbs and 1 tablespoon of melted butter until combined well, then distribute evenly over the vegetables with mixture.
Put in oven and bake for 25 to 30 minutes or until hot and bubbly and the crumbs have browned some.
Remove and allow to cool for a few minutes, then serve warm.
Makes 4 to 6 servings.

Cucumber Ginger Salad

2 large cucumbers, peeled
1/3 cup rice vinegar
4 tsp white sugar
1 tsp kosher salt
1 1/2 tsp minced fresh ginger root

Cut cucumbers in half lengthwise and remove any large seeds and extra pulpy flesh if necessary.
Slice into very thin pieces, crosswise, into crescent shapes.
In a bowl whisk together the vinegar, sugar, salt, and ginger.
Add the cucumbers to the bowl and toss together until well coated.
Cover and refrigerate for at least an hour before serving so the flavors blend well.

Curried Carrot Raisin Compote

2 Tbsp cooking oil
1 small yellow onion, diced
4 garlic cloves, minced
1 tsp mustard seeds
2 Tbsp raisins
1/2 lemon, zested and squeezed
2 Tbsp curry powder
3 carrots, medium size, coarse chopped
2 cups vegetable or chicken stock
1 Tbsp honey

In a large skillet, heat the oil over medium heat and cook onions until softened, then add the garlic and mustard seeds and heat until garlic is fragrant, about 1 minute.
Add the raisins, lemon zest and juice, and stir together, heating for about 1 minute.
Add the curry powder, carrots, stock and honey and stir together, bringing to a boil briefly.
Turn heat to low, cover, and simmer slowly and gently for about 30 to 40 minutes or until carrots are tender.
Serve over brown rice.

Damson Plum Pudding With Butter Sauce

1/2 cup butter
1 cup sugar
3 eggs, beaten
1 cup Damson plum pulp
1 cup flour
1/2 tsp cinnamon
1 tsp baking soda
1/4 tsp nutmeg
3 Tbsp buttermilk

Sauce:
1 cup Damson plum juice
1/2 cup water
2 tsp cornstarch
1 cup sugar
2 Tbsp butter

Preheat oven to 350 degrees and lightly grease an 8 x 8 baking pan.
In a mixer or food processor, put the butter and sugar and set to cream until light, fluffy, and light yellow color.
With mixer running slowly, add eggs and plum pulp and blend just until combined.
In separate bowl, sift together the flour, cinnamon, baking soda, and nutmeg, then, with mixer running slowly, start adding dry ingredients alternating with buttermilk, until blended together.
Pour the mixture into prepared baking pan and bake in preheated oven at 350 degrees for 20 or 25 minutes or until pudding is set and not liquid in the middle.
Remove from oven and let cool slightly, then cut into serving size pieces and serve on individual plates with sauce drizzled on top.

To make sauce:
Put plum juice and water in a saucepan and put over medium heat.
In separate bowl, mix together the cornstarch and sugar; take a couple tablespoons of liquid from the pan and stir into the cornstarch and sugar mixture, then put all into the saucepan with the liquid.
Stir together in saucepan over heat until mixture thickens, then add butter, stir until melted and hot, then pour over prepared pudding squares on plates.

Date Walnut Sweet Bread

1 cup chopped dates
1 cup boiling water
1 Tbsp vegetable oil
1 cup brown sugar, packed
1 egg
1 tsp vanilla extract
2 cups all-purpose flour
1 tsp baking soda
1/4 tsp salt
1 cup chopped walnuts

Preheat oven to 350 degrees and lightly grease a loaf pan.
In a heat-resistant bowl, put the dates, boiling water, and oil, stir gently and let sit for 10 minutes.
To the bowl (do NOT drain off liquid) add the brown sugar, egg, and vanilla extract, stir to combine well.
In a separate bowl, stir together the dry ingredients (flour, baking soda, and salt) then sprinkle in date mixture, stirring as you do to combine, but do not over-mix.
Add walnuts and fold in with big spatula.
Turn the batter into your prepared loaf pan and bake in preheated oven at 350 degrees for 60 to 65 minutes or until top is lightly golden brown.
Remove and cool in loaf pan on countertop for 5 to 10 minutes, then slide out onto cooling rack.

Dixie Meets Italy Collard Greens

1/2 pound collard greens
1 tsp olive oil
1 cup rough chopped celery
3/4 cup rough chopped onion
2 cloves garlic, minced
1 can (14 oz size) stewed tomatoes, undrained
2 tsp Italian seasoning (may substitute a mixture of equal parts oregano OR basil, and marjoram, rosemary, and thyme)
1 can (15 oz size) cannellini beans (may substitute navy or Great Northern), rinsed and drained

Sort and trim the collard greens to remove any browned parts and tough stems; wash thoroughly by soaking in cold fresh water, then rinsing under running water; drain, then coarsely chop and allow to drain in colander.
In a large soup pot over medium heat, put the celery and cook for 3 minutes, add onion and cook for another 3 minutes, then add garlic and cook for 1 minute, stirring constantly.
Add the prepared collard greens to the pot, stir, then add the stewed tomatoes with their juice and the seasoning; cook stirring to combine just until the collard greens wilt. Reduce heat to low, cover the pot and simmer slowly for 15 minutes.
Add beans, stir, cover the pot and simmer slowly for 5 more minutes.
Serve alongside your main meat dish or as a meal on its own with good crusty bread to sop up the juice.
This makes 4 servings.

Durian Fruit Puree Cheesecake

1 (9 inch) prepared graham cracker crust
2 ounces cream cheese, room temperature
7 fluid ounces sweetened condensed milk
1/4 cup pureed fresh durian
2 eggs
1/2 cup sour cream
1 tsp vanilla extract
1 Tbsp durian or banana extract

Preheat oven to 325 degrees.
Put the cream cheese in mixing bowl and beat until fluffy.
With beaters running, pour in the sweetened condensed milk and continue beating until blended well and smooth.
With beaters running, slowly add the pureed durian, then the eggs, sour cream, vanilla extract, and durian or banana extract, continue running beaters until blended well.
Pour the mixture into the graham cracker crust.
Bake in preheated oven for 55 to 65 minutes until the filling is set and edges are starting to pull away a bit and are lightly browned.
Remove and allow to cool slightly before serving warm. You may also chill in the refrigerator overnight and serve cold.

Garden Corn Souffle

2 cups corn, fresh cut from cob
2 eggs
2 Tbsp butter, melted
2 cups milk, scalded
1 small red or green bell pepper, finely diced
2 Tbsp grated sweet onion
1 tsp kosher salt
1/8 tsp freshly ground black pepper

Preheat oven to 325 degrees. Lightly grease a 1 1/2 quart casserole dish. Set a larger baking dish out (that the casserole will fit in). You will be baking the casserole in a water bath in the larger dish.
With a sharp knife, cut corn kernels from cob (stand corn cob on its tip, holding by large stem end, and run knife blade from top to bottom, removing kernels.)
In a cold mixing bowl, beat eggs until frothy, then whisk in milk and melted butter until blended.
Put corn, bell pepper, onion, salt, and black pepper in bowl with egg mixture and stir to combine.
Pour the mixture into the casserole and set it in the larger baking dish and set in oven, then fill a pitcher with hot water from faucet and pour carefully into larger baking dish so casserole is sitting in a water bath inside the oven. Slide all the way into the preheated oven and bake at 325 degrees for 55 to 65 minutes.
Test to see if done by inserting a thin knife blade into center; it should come out clean if the eggs are set.
Remove and let stand at room temperature for 5 to 10 minutes before serving.
This will serve about 4 to 6 people as a side dish.

Garden Cucumber Salsa

6 small cucumbers, peeled and finely chopped
3 medium Roma tomatoes, finely chopped
1 small green bell pepper, finely chopped
1 jalapeno pepper, seeded and minced
1 small onion, diced small
1 clove garlic, minced
2 Tbsp lime juice
1 tsp minced fresh parsley
2 tsp minced fresh cilantro
1/2 tsp dried dill weed
1/2 tsp salt

Put all the ingredients in a large glass or plastic bowl and stir to combine. Cover and refrigerate for at least 1 hour . Serve with tortilla chips.

Kid Krazy Cabbage Casserole

1 large head cabbage, shredded (about 12 cups)
1 onion, chopped
6 Tbsp butter, divided
1 can (10 oz size) cream of mushroom soup, undiluted
8 ounces process cheese (American style, or Velveeta), cubed
salt and pepper to taste
1/4 cup dry bread crumbs

Preheat oven to 350 degrees.
Put cabbage in a large pot and fill about 1/4 full with fresh water; put over medium high heat and bring to a boil, cooking until cabbage is just tender, then drain thoroughly.
In a large skillet, add 5 tablespoons of the butter and the onions; cook over medium heat until onions are soft, then stir in the soup, add the cheese and stir until the cheese melts; remove from heat.
Add the cooked cabbage, salt, and pepper, tossing to combine.
Turn out into a large casserole dish.
In a small pot or skillet, melt the remaining 1 tablespoon butter and stir in the bread crumbs; sprinkle this mixture over the cabbage in casserole.
Bake, uncovered, in preheated oven at 350 degrees for 25 to 35 minutes or until top gets browned and casserole is hot all the way through.
This makes about 6 to 8 servings as a side dish.

Laotian Durian Fruit And Rice Dessert

1 cup sticky rice
1 1/2 cup fresh coconut milk, divided
1 cup mashed durian fruit
1 to 2 Tbsp sugar (to taste)

Rinse the sticky rice in fresh water and drain in sieve or colander.
Put sticky rice and 1 cup of coconut milk in a saucepan over high heat, bring to a boil, then turn to low and simmer for 45 minutes.
In a bowl put the durian fruit and add about 1 to 2 Tbsp of sugar to taste and mix well.
Divide the rice between two serving bowls.
Spoon the durian mixture over the steamed rice dividing evenly between the two bowls.
Pour half the remaining fresh coconut milk into each serving bowl.
This is a Laotian dessert that will be well received by anyone with a sweet tooth.
Serves 2 and can be doubled, tripled, etc.

Meaty Stewed Cabbage

1 lb. bulk pork sausage
1 lb. ground beef
1 large onion, chopped
1 can (28 oz) diced tomatoes
1 can (6 oz) tomato paste
2 Tbsp apple cider vinegar
1 Tbsp chili powder
1 tsp garlic powder
1/8 tsp red pepper flakes
10 to 12 cups shredded cabbage (depending on how much cabbage you want)

In a large Dutch oven over medium heat, put the sausage and beef, cook (breaking up the meat) until browned slightly.
Add the remaining ingredients to pot and allow to come up to a boil, then immediately reduce heat and simmer, covered with lid vented slightly, for 10 to 15 minutes or until cabbage is tender.
Will serve 8 hungry people or 10 to 12 light eaters.

Mediterranean Collards

1 lb. collard greens, trimmed, rinsed, rough chopped
2 cups water
1 Tbsp olive oil
1 small yellow onion, diced
8 cloves garlic, minced
1 Tbsp olive oil
1 green bell pepper, diced
1 Tbsp fresh lemon juice
1 tsp salt
1/2 tsp ground turmeric
1/2 tsp paprika
1/2 tsp ground allspice
2 Tbsp minced fresh ginger root

Put prepared collard greens in a large pot with the 2 cups of water over medium-high heat and bring to a boil; immediately reduce heat to low, cover and simmer for about 15 to 20 minutes or until collards are tender. Drain over a bowl, reserving the cooking water; set aside both the collards and the drained water.
In same large pot, put the olive oil and onions over medium heat and cook until onions become clear and just start to brown, then stir in the garlic and cook for 1 minute.
Throw in the collards, and another 1 tablespoon of olive oil and the reserved cooking water and cook over medium heat (uncovered) until the cooking liquid almost disappears entirely, about 10 to 12 minutes should do it.
Put the diced green bell pepper in the pot and add the remaining ingredients, stir and simmer over medium-low heat until the peppers soften, about 5 minutes. Serve warm.
Serves 6 people as a side dish.

Mozzarella Swiss Chard Wrap Snacks

8 large Swiss chard leaves
1 large (or 2 medium) ripe tomato, cut into 8 wedges
2 Tbsp olive oil
1 Tbsp onion flakes
salt and pepper
1/2 cup grated Mozzarella cheese

Preheat oven to 400 degrees and lightly oil a large baking sheet.
Put big pot of water on stove and bring to a boil; drop Swiss chard leaves in for about 30 seconds, just long enough to soften, remove and drain on rack.
Lay leaves out on prepared baking pan and brush each with olive oil lightly.
Place a tomato wedge in the center of each leaf, sprinkle with a little onion flakes, season with salt and pepper, then divide the mozzarella cheese evenly on top of each leaf.
Roll the leaves up and over the tomato and cheese, tucking under to close.
Place in preheated oven at 400 degrees and cook for 10 to 15 minutes or until cheese is melted and Swiss chard is starting to brown around the edges.

Savory Sweet Cranberry Ginger Chutney

1 Tbsp olive oil
1/4 cup finely minced shallot
1 Tbsp finely grated fresh ginger
1 bag (12 oz size) fresh cranberries, rinsed and sorted
1 cup sugar
2 Tbsp red wine vinegar
1 cup water
kosher salt and ground pepper

Put oil in a large saucepan over medium-low heat.
Add the shallots and ginger and cook until shallots are soft, about 4 to 5 minutes, stirring occasionally.
Add the cleaned cranberries, sugar, red wine vinegar, and water and bring the mixture to a boil, reduce heat immediately and simmer slowly for about 10 to 15 minutes, stirring often.
The berries will soften and split and the mixture will thicken.
Add salt and pepper, taste, adjust, and remove from heat.
This may be served at room temperature or chilled in the refrigerator.
Serve alongside grilled pork, roast chicken, turkey, or other meats.

Sicilian Cauliflower Olio Pasta

1 large or 2 medium heads cauliflower, cleaned and cut into small florettes
salt
6 Tbsp extra-virgin olive oil
1 medium onion, finely diced
dash red pepper flakes
4 anchovy fillets, chopped
1/4 cup pine nuts
1/4 cup raisins
1 pound Fusilli or Penne pasta (or other if preferred)

Fill a large pot with water and put on stove; bring to a boil, then carefully add cauliflower and cook, boiling steady but not too hard, for about 5 minutes or until cauliflower is just fork tender. Remove the cauliflower with a slotted spoon to a colander (reserve the cooking water in the pot.)
In a different large pot over medium-low heat, add the olive oil, onion, and red pepper flakes and cook, stirring, until onion softens.
Remove the onion pot from the heat and add the anchovy fillets, stirring quickly to incorporate them in onion and olive oil; the anchovies should dissolve somewhat. (Be sure you do not do this over the heat – anchovies can burn easily.)
Put the pot back on medium-low heat and add the pine nuts, raisins, and cauliflower, stirring to heat through, about 2 to 3 minutes.
Anchovies often have enough salt, but taste and add salt if flavor isn't what you desire.
You can add a tablespoon or more of the cauliflower cooking water if the sauce seems too dry or thick, stir and set aside, covering to keep warm.
Meanwhile, bring the stockpot of cauliflower cooking water back to a boil to cook pasta in (add more water if necessary before boiling.) Cook pasta according to package directions.
Drain well and dump pasta into pot with cauliflower and toss to combine.
Let sit to absorb flavors for about 5 minutes, stir again and serve warm or room temperature. Sprinkle with grated fresh Parmesan if desired.
This will serve about 2 hungry people, or 4 if part of larger meal.

Smokin Beef Celery Sticks

1 (8 oz) package dried smoked beef or turkey, chopped small
1 (8 oz) package cream cheese, softened
3 Tbsp prepared horseradish
1/4 tsp ground black pepper
1 tsp lemon juice
1 bunch celery

Put the chopped up beef and cream cheese in a bowl and using a fork, blend until mixed together well. Add the horseradish, black pepper, and lemon juice and mash together until smooth.
Cover and refrigerate to let flavors mix for about 1 hour.
Clean celery sticks and cut into snack size 'logs' about 2 bites size.
Remove cream cheese spread from refrigerator and allow to sit at room temperature for a couple minutes, then stir again.
Spread cream cheese mixture into the celery stalks and serve as a snack.
You'll have enough celery sticks to serve about 6 to 10 people, depending on the situation.

Swiss Chard Italian Lasagna

1 lb lasagna noodles, uncooked
8 oz sweet Italian sausage
1 large yellow onion, diced
2 Tbsp chopped sun dried tomatoes, soaked in 4 Tbsp water
2 tsp dried crushed basil
4 cups (32 oz) tomato sauce
1/4 cup good dry red wine
1 large bunch fresh Swiss chard, trimmed, coarse chopped, washed
1 lb Ricotta
1 lb Mozzarella, shredded
1/2 cup freshly grated Parmesan
salt and pepper to taste

Preheat oven to 350 degrees and lightly grease a lasagna baking pan (about 9 1/2 x 14 if you have one; if not a 9x13.) Note: you are using uncooked noodles in this lasagna. There is plenty of liquid to cook the noodles right in the dish.

Prepare the sauce: Break up or cut up the sausage small and put in skillet over medium-high heat and brown.
Reduce the heat to medium-low and add the onion, cooking until softened, about 3 to 4 minutes.
Add the sun-dried tomatoes, along with the liquid they soaked in, and the basil, stir and cook for 1 minute.
Add the tomato sauce and red wine, bring just to a bubble, reduce the heat to low and simmer for 15 minutes, stirring occasionally. Taste and add salt and pepper as desired.

Prepare the Swiss chard: After trimming off all the stems, washing and chopping, wilt the leaves by quickly stir-frying them in a large skillet with a drizzle of olive oil over medium-high heat. Do not over cook, just cook until beginning to wilt, then remove and let drain in colander. (Do this in two batches if your skillet is too crowded.)

Put together lasagna in pan:
First layer: single layer noodles, 1/3 ricotta, 1/3 Swiss chard, 1/4 Parmesan, 1/4 sauce, 1/4 Mozzarella
Repeat: single layer noodles, 1/3 ricotta, 1/3 Swiss chard, 1/4 Parmesan, 1/4 sauce, 1/4 Mozzarella
Repeat: single layer noodles, 1/3 ricotta, 1/3 Swiss chard, 1/4 Parmesan, 1/4 sauce, 1/4 Mozzarella
Final layer: single layer noodles, 1/4 sauce, 1/4 Parmesan, 1/4 Mozzarella, sprinkle with a little dried basil if desired.
Cover the pan with aluminum foil, sealing well.
Bake in the preheated oven at 350 degrees for 1 hour. Uncover and check to see if the liquid has been absorbed. If not, return to oven, covered loosely this time with the foil, and bake another 10 minutes, check again and cook an additional 5 minutes if the lasagna is still too watery. (Some liquid will absorb while it stands out to cool.)

Remove and let stand at room temperature, covered loosely with foil, for about 10 minutes to let the lasagna 'set up' so it won't fall apart when you cut it.

www.ingramcontent.com/pod-product-compliance
Lightning Source LLC
Chambersburg PA
CBHW081628100526
44590CB00021B/3646